ESSENTIAL SIGHT-SINGING

VOLUME 2

By Emily Crocker
and John Leavitt

ISBN 978-1-4234-1003-4

HAL•LEONARD®
CORPORATION

7777 W. BLUEMOUND RD. P.O. BOX 13819 MILWAUKEE, WI 53213

Visit Hal Leonard Online at
www.halleonard.com

PREFACE

Essential Sight-Singing was adapted from the *Essential Musicianship* books from the *Essential Elements for Choir* choral textbook series in order to bring the most successful aspects of the program into the hands of more choral singers.

It is designed to provide a basis for developing music literacy within the choral rehearsal through sequential development of music reading skills. Choirs are encouraged to spend 10–15 minutes per hour of rehearsal, including practice/review and introducing new material.

Choirs and singers are encouraged to use a systematic method for sight-reading pitch and rhythm. Several methods are outlined in the appendix of this volume.

For pitch reading:
Solfège (movable do)
Solfège (fixed do)
Numbers

For rhythm reading:
Kodály
Traditional
Eastman System

Choose the method based on the age/experience of the singers, methods used by other organizations in your school or district, methods familiar to your students, or your own background or training. Remember, it is not *which* method you use, but rather that it is employed consistently and regularly.

The exercises and songs in this volume are structured to allow students to discover their individual potential. The material is score oriented so that students are led to discover the meaning of music both through experiencing it and interpreting it through the medium of the printed page. This process of converting symbol to sound and sound to symbol is at the heart of becoming a musically literate individual.

Also available is an Accompaniment CD that provides light accompaniment for the combinable pitch builders, speech choruses and songs. In keeping with the spirit of sight-reading, there is no singing on the CD. Unless otherwise noted, starting pitches and one full measure of beats are provided before each pitch builder and a cappella song.

Good luck!

~Emily Crocker and John Leavitt, authors

1.1 Beat and Rhythm

Rhythm is the organization of sound length (duration).

Beat is a steadily recurring pulse.

Rhythm Practice

Practice keeping a steady beat as a group. Clap, tap, or chant with a clock or metronome.

Note Values

Three common note values are the *quarter note,* the *half note,* and the *whole note.*

Quarter Note   Half Note   Whole Note

In most of the music that we'll begin with, the quarter note will be assigned the beat.

You'll notice from the chart below that *two quarter notes* have the same duration as *one half note,* and that *two half notes* (or four quarter notes) have the same duration as *one whole note.*

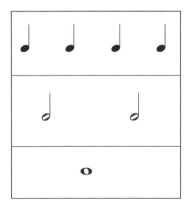

1.2 Rhythm Builder

Read each line (clap, tap, or chant). Concentrate on keeping a steady beat. Repeat as necessary until you've mastered the exercise.

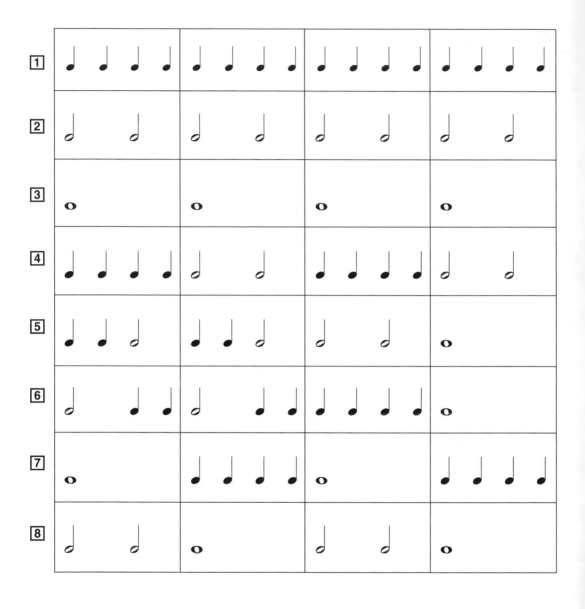

1.3 Basic Notation

A *staff* is a graph of 5 lines and 4 spaces on which music is written. The staff shown below is a grand staff. A *grand staff* is a grouping of two staves.

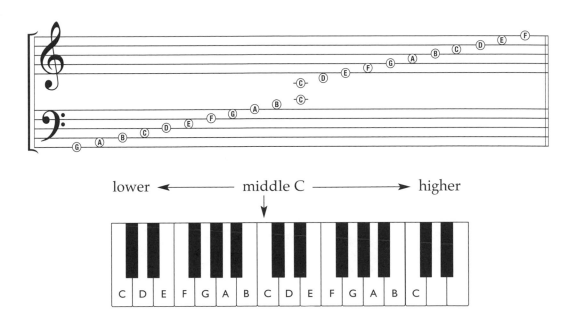

Notice the two symbols at the beginning of the staves on the left hand side. These are called clefs. A *clef* is a symbol that identifies a set of pitches. The *Treble Clef* generally refers to pitches higher than middle C. The *Bass Clef* generally refers to pitches lower than middle C. Notice that middle C has its own little line and may be written in either clef – either at the bottom of the treble clef or the top of the bass clef.

Treble Clef (G Clef)
Second line is G
(The curve of the clef
loops around the G line).

Bass Clef (F Clef)
Fourth line is F
(The dots of the clef
surround the F line).

1.4 Measures, Meters & Barlines

Barlines are vertical lines that divide the staff into smaller sections called *measures*. A *double barline* indicates the end of a section or piece of music.

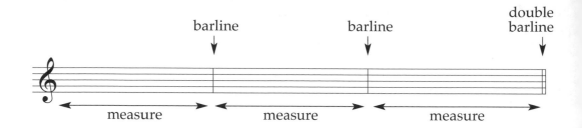

Meter is a form of rhythmic organization. For example:

4 = Four beats per measure (♩ ♩ ♩ ♩).
4 = The quarter note (♩) receives the beat.

3 = Three beats per measure (♩ ♩ ♩).
4 = The quarter note (♩) receives the beat.

2 = Two beats per measure (♩ ♩).
4 = The quarter note (♩) receives the beat.

The numbers that identify the meter are called the *time signature*. The time signature is placed after the clef at the beginning of a song or section of a song.

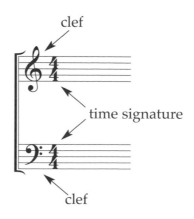

1.5 Rhythm Builder

Read each line (clap, tap, or chant).

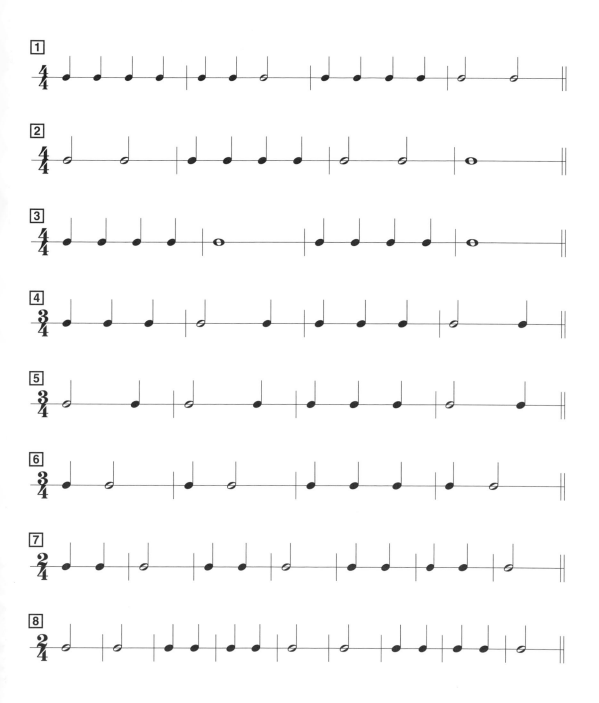

2.1 Pitch, Scale & Key of C

Pitch – The highness or lowness of musical sound.

Scale – An inventory or collection of pitches. The word "scale" (from the Italian *scala*) means "ladder." Thus, many musical scales are a succession of pitches higher and lower.

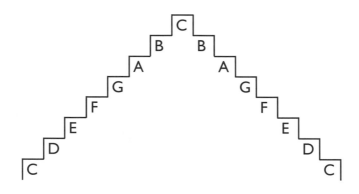

Key – The importance of one pitch over the others in a scale. Frequently, the key-note or tone might be described as the home tone. In the key of C, C is the home tone or keynote.

Key of C Scale

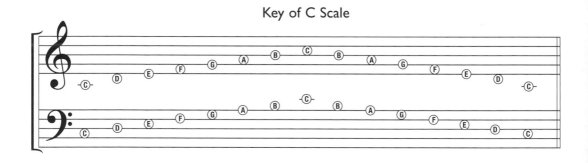

2.2 Pitch Builder

Identify the following pitches in the key of C. Echo sing or sing as a group.

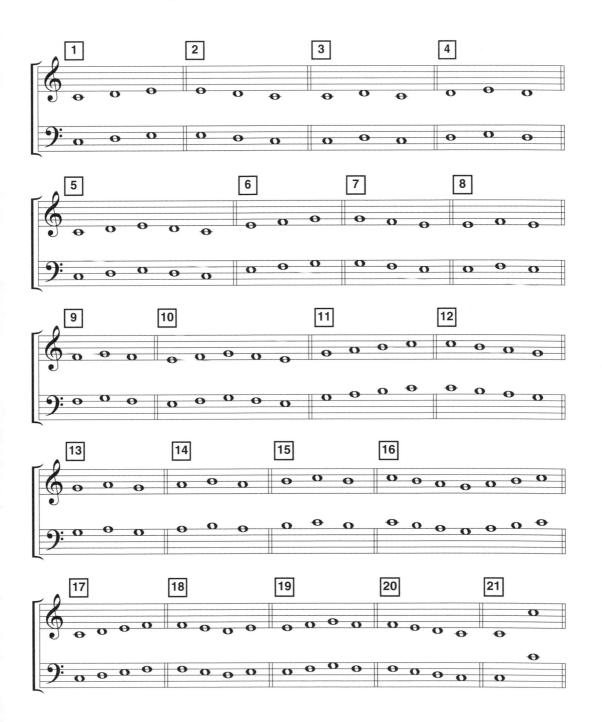

2.3 Pitch Builder

The following exercises combine pitch and rhythm. Chant the rhythm first, then add pitch. Repeat as necessary. When you've mastered all the exercises, you may sing the lines in any combination. For example, divide into two groups with one group singing #1 and the other group singing #2.

Each line sung by itself produces *melody* (a succession of musical tones). When two or more melodies are combined, the result is *harmony* (musical tones sounded simultaneously).

2.4 Sight-Read

Apply what you've learned about music reading to this short song.
- Chant the rhythm.
- Add pitch. Repeat as necessary for accuracy.
- Sing with text and expression.

Tr. #2 Sweet Music in the Night

for 2-Part Mixed and Piano

Words and Music by
EMILY CROCKER

3.1 Whole Steps and Half Steps

Remember the *key* is the importance of one pitch over the others in a scale. The keynote is described as the home tone. The *key of C* played on the piano would begin on C and progress stepwise using only the white keys of the piano.

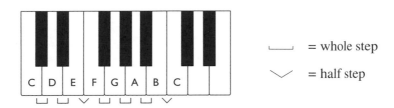

These steps on the piano for the key of C are an arrangement of whole steps and half steps.

- A *half step* is the smallest distance (or interval) between two notes on a keyboard.
- A *whole step* is the combination of two half steps side by side.
- A *major scale* is a specific arrangement of whole steps and half steps in the following order:

C Major Scale

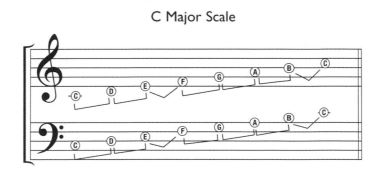

3.2 Pitch Builder

Singing in Parts

Human voices are generally divided into four basic ranges:

Soprano - the highest treble voice, usually written in treble clef

Alto - a treble voice that is lower than the soprano, usually written in treble clef

Tenor - a high male voice written in bass clef or treble clef

Bass - a male voice written in bass clef that is lower than the tenor

Sing each line separately and in any combination.

In the example below, the lines are combined. Notice how the parts are bracketed together.

3.3 Ledger Lines

Middle C can be written on its own short line in either clef. Other pitches may also be written that way. These short lines are called *ledger lines*. Ledger lines may be used to represent notes either above or below the staff. On the staff below, notes connected by arrows are the same pitch.

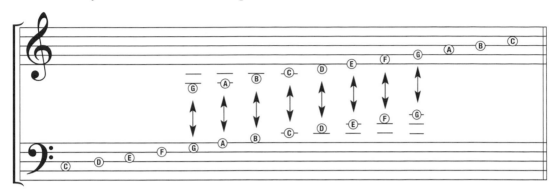

Identify the following pitches in the key of C. Echo sing or sing as a group.

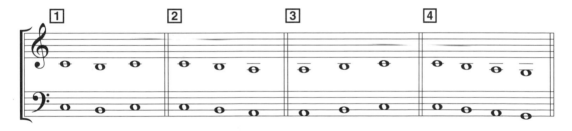

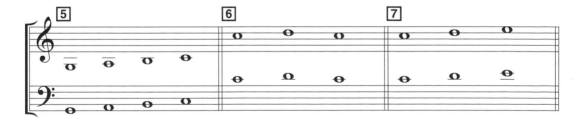

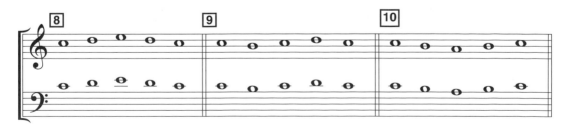

3.4 Sight-Read

Tr. #4 Kyrie Eleison

for SATB, a cappella

Traditional Latin

Music by
JOHN LEAVITT

4.1 Sharps and Flats

You'll recall the order of whole and half steps for the C major scale:

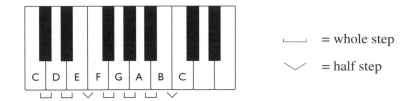

        ⌐─┐ = whole step
        ⌄   = half step

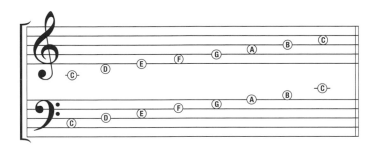

Music may be written with any note being the keynote. Because the order of whole and half steps must always be followed regardless of the keynote, the need arises for *sharps* (♯) and *flats* (♭).

A *sharp* raises the pitch one half step. These notes, F♯ (F sharp), would be written with the sharp sign to the left of the noteheads.

A *flat* lowers the pitch one half step. These notes, B♭ (B flat), would be written with the flat sign to the left of the noteheads.

4.2 Key of G Major

To build a major scale starting on G, using the same arrangement of whole steps and half steps as in the key of C major, you'll notice the need for an F♯.

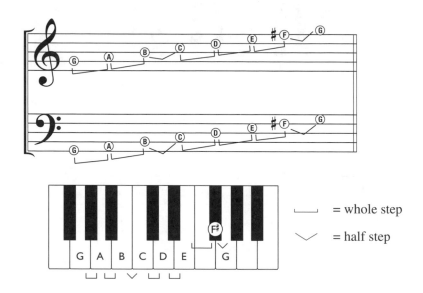

= whole step

= half step

If we had written F - G, the *interval* (distance) between these two pitches would have been a whole step rather than the required half step.

Key of G Practice

Practice singing the G major scale. In each clef, two octaves of this scale are written below. Because of the wider range, you may only be able to sing a portion of the two octaves, but take note of your own vocal range. What is your lowest note? Your highest note?

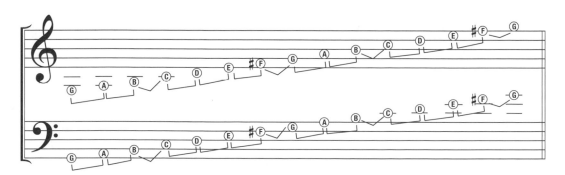

4.3 Pitch Builder

Identify the following pitches in the key of G major. Echo sing or sing as a group.

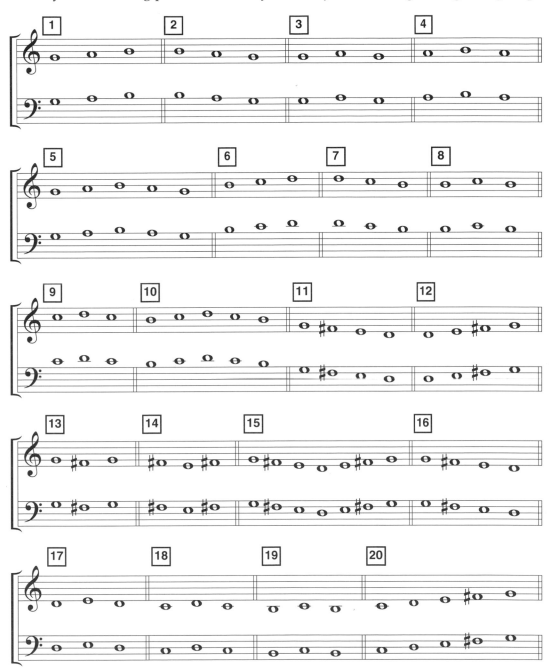

4.4 Accidentals and Key Signature

A *sharp* raises the pitch one half step. These notes, F♯ (F sharp), would be written with the sharp sign to the left of the noteheads.

A *flat* lowers the pitch one half step. These notes, B♭ (B flat), would be written with the flat sign to the left of the noteheads.

There are two ways to write sharps and flats in music. One way is to write the sharp or flat to the left of the noteheads as shown above. These are called *accidentals* because they are not normally found in the key in which you are performing.

The other way is to write a *key signature*. Since we know that the key of G major will always use an F♯, rather than write the sharp sign on every F in the song, we simply write a sharp on F's line at the beginning of the song right after the clef sign(s) and before the time signature. (Note: The key signature is used with every clef sign in the song as a reminder).

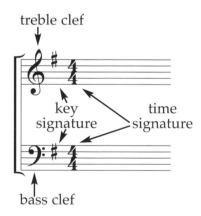

Placing an F♯ in the key signature indicates that the music is in the key of *G major* which always uses an F♯. Remember that the key of *C major* has no sharps or flats. Thus, the absence of sharps or flats in the key signature indicates that the music is in the key of C major.

4.5 Pitch Builder

Sing each line separately and in any combination.

4.6 Sight-Read

Tr. #6 Sun Is High

for 4-Part Mixed, a cappella

Text by
LOWELL MASON (1850)

Music by
JOHN LEAVITT

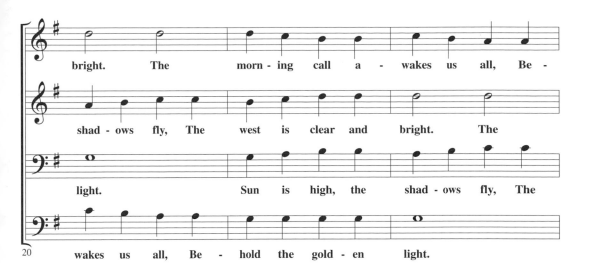

bright. The morn-ing call a - wakes us all, Be -

shad - ows fly, The west is clear and bright. The

light. Sun is high, the shad - ows fly, The

wakes us all, Be - hold the gold - en light.

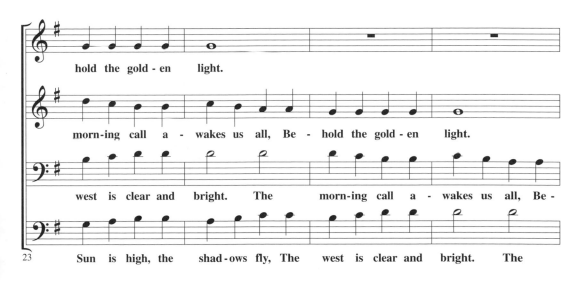

hold the gold - en light.

morn - ing call a - wakes us all, Be - hold the gold - en light.

west is clear and bright. The morn-ing call a - wakes us all, Be -

Sun is high, the shad - ows fly, The west is clear and bright. The

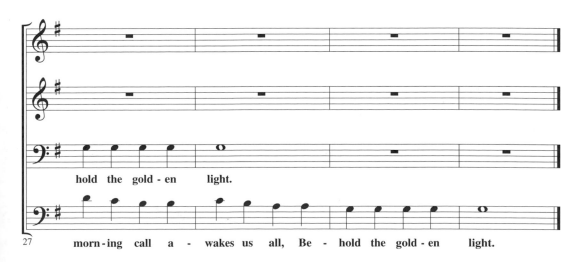

hold the gold - en light.

morn - ing call a - wakes us all, Be - hold the gold - en light.

5.1 Melodic Intervals

An *interval* is the measurement of distance between two pitches. When intervals are played in succession, they are called *melodic intervals.* Following are examples of intervals of 2nds, 3rds, 4ths, and 5ths.

Read the pitches, echo sing, or sing each example as a group:

5.2 Pitch Builder

Practice the following exercises. Echo sing or sing as a group.

5.3 Harmonic Intervals

To review, an *interval* is the measurement between two pitches. When intervals are played in succession, they are called *melodic intervals.*

When intervals are played simultaneously, they are called *harmonic intervals.* Here are some examples of harmonic intervals.

Harmonic intervals are the building blocks of harmony. Two or more harmonic intervals combined form a chord. Thus, a *chord* is the combination of three or more tones played simultaneously. Here are some examples of chords.

5.4 Pitch Builder

Practice the following exercises. Notice the harmonic intervals that result when one part sustains a pitch while the other part moves to a higher or lower pitch. Listen carefully for balance, tuning, and blend.

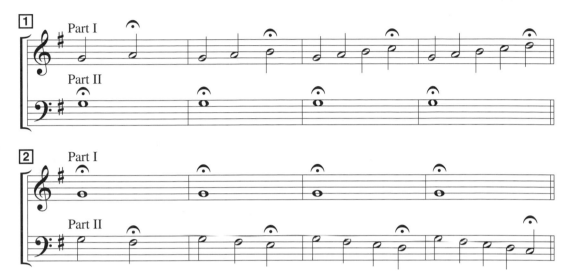

Practice the following exercises in three parts. Notice the chord that results as one part sustains a pitch while the other parts move higher and lower.

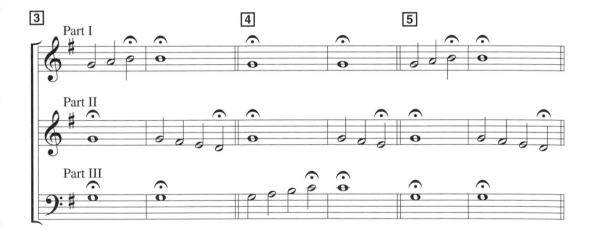

5.5 Pitch Builder

Sing each line separately and in any combination.

5.6 Sight-Read

Tr. #8 ## The Spider and the Fly

for SATB and Piano

Traditional text, adapted

Music by
EMILY CROCKER

6.1 The Tonic Chord

Two or more harmonic intervals combined form a chord. A *chord* is the combination of three or more tones played or sung simultaneously.

A *triad* is a special type of three-note chord built in thirds over a *root tone*. Following are some examples of triads.

Triads

When a *triad* is built on the keynote of a major scale it is called a *tonic chord*. You'll notice that the word "tonic" is related to the word "tone." "Tonic" is another way of referring to the keynote of a major scale, and "tonic chord" is another way of referring to the triad built on that keynote.

Tonic Chord: C Major

Tonic Chord: G Major

6.2 Pitch Builder

Practice the following drills which outline the tonic chord. Remember, when the melody outlines the tonic chord, you are singing melodic intervals. When three or more parts sing the pitches of the tonic chord simultaneously, the ensemble is singing a chord.

Tonic Drill

Melody Drill

Chord Builders

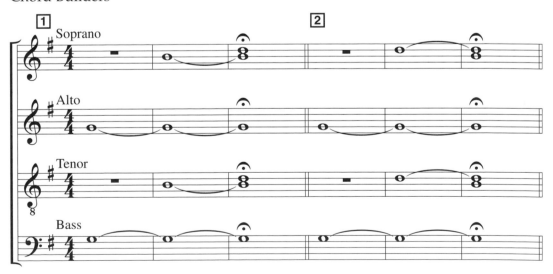

6.3 Pitch Builder

Sing each line separately and in any combination.

6.4 Rests

Rests are silences in music. They come in a variety of lengths, just like notes. These silences are just as important as the notes.

	notes	rests
whole	𝅝	▬
half	𝅗𝅥	▬
quarter	♩	𝄽

Rests and notes of the same name share the same duration.

6.5 Rhythm Builder

Read each line (clap, tap, or chant).

6.6 Pitch Builder

Sing each line separately and in any combination.

6.7 Sight-Read

Tr. #11 To Make a Prairie

for SATB, a cappella

Poem by
EMILY DICKINSON

Music by
EMILY CROCKER

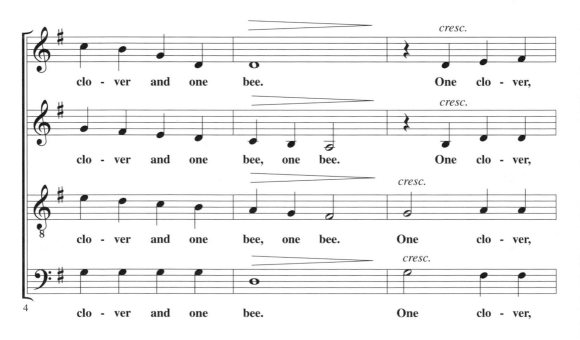

6.8 Sight-Read

Tr. #12 How Doth the Little Crocodile

(from "Alice's Adventures in Wonderland")

for SATB and Piano

Poem by
LEWIS CARROLL

Music by
JOHN LEAVITT

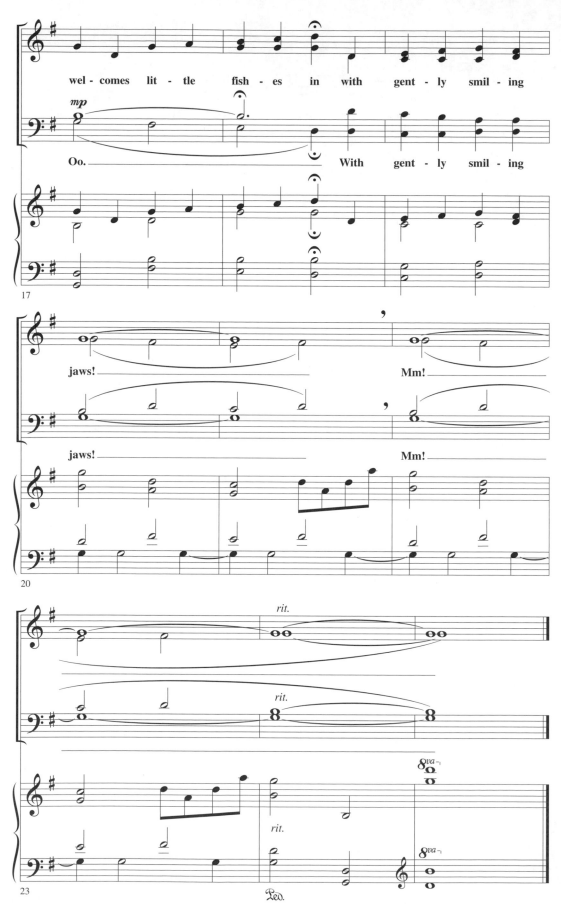

7.1 Changing Meters

Remember that *meter* is a form of rhythmic organization. In the simple meters we have been using, the top number indicates the number of beats per measure in the music. The bottom number indicates which note value receives the beat.

$\frac{4}{4}$ = Four beats per measure (♩ ♩ ♩ ♩).
= The quarter note (♩) receives the beat.

$\frac{3}{4}$ = Three beats per measure (♩ ♩ ♩).
= The quarter note (♩) receives the beat.

$\frac{2}{4}$ = Two beats per measure (♩ ♩).
= The quarter note (♩) receives the beat.

So that the ear can easily recognize and group notes into the various meters, each meter stresses certain beats. Almost all meters stress the first beat of each measure. This is called the *downbeat*.

In $\frac{4}{4}$ meter, a secondary stress occurs on beat three, along with the stressed downbeat.

7.2 Rhythm Builder

Read the following exercise with changing meters.

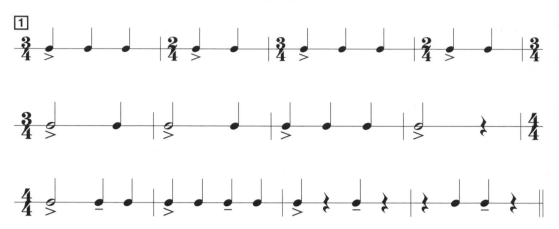

Dotted Half Notes

In music notation, we need to be able to measure note values with durations of three beats (especially in meters of 3). Our notational system accomplishes this by adding a dot to the right of a notehead. The rule governing dotted notes is the dot receives *half the value of the note to which it is attached.*

$$\frac{3}{4}\ \text{♩} = 2\ \text{beats} \qquad \frac{3}{4}\ \text{♩.} = 3\ \text{beats}$$

Practice the following exercise in $\frac{3}{4}$ meter:

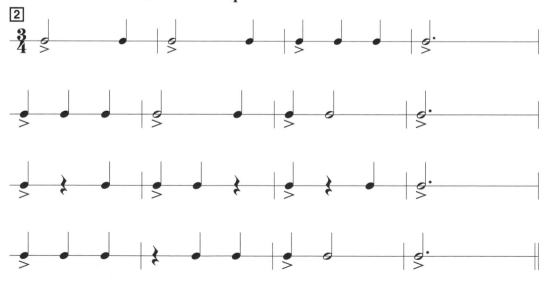

7.3 Pitch Builder

Read each line separately and in any combination.

7.4 Sight-Read

Tr. #14 Three Nursery Rhymes

I. Humpty Dumpty

for Unison Voices and Piano

Traditional Rhyme

Music by
EMILY CROCKER

Tr. #15 II. A Diller, A Dollar

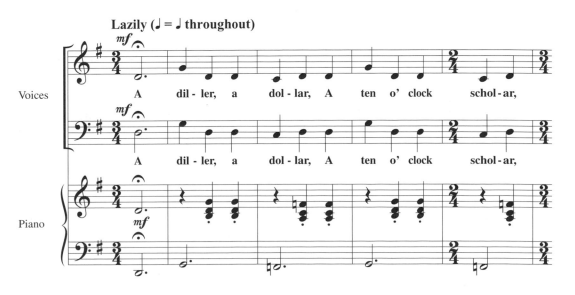

What makes you come so soon? You used to come at ten o' clock, but now you come at noon!

III. Jack and Jill

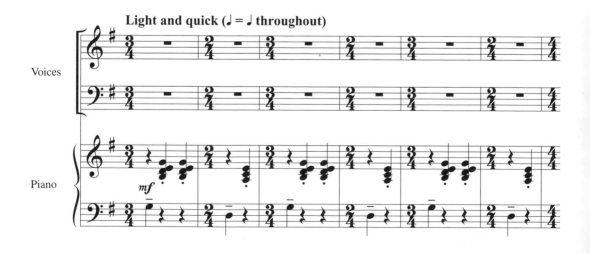

Light and quick (♩ = ♩ throughout)

Voices

Piano

8.1 Eighth Notes and Rests

So far, we've used whole, half, and quarter notes. An *eighth note* (♪) is half the value of a quarter note. Two eighth notes (♫) have the same duration as one quarter note. The eighth note has a corresponding rest, the eighth rest (ᵞ), which shares the same length as an eighth note.

Below is a chart summarizing the notes and rests we've learned.

	notes	rests
whole	𝅝	▬
half	𝅗𝅥	▬
quarter	𝅘𝅥	𝄽
eighth	𝅘𝅥𝅮	ᵞ

The following diagram summarizes the relationships between the notes we've studied:

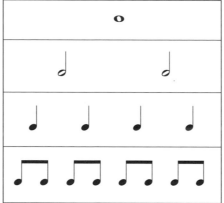

If the quarter note receives the beat, you can consider eighth notes to be a *division* of the beat:

Beat: 𝅘𝅥 𝅘𝅥 𝅘𝅥 𝅘𝅥

Division: 𝅘𝅥𝅮𝅘𝅥𝅮 𝅘𝅥𝅮𝅘𝅥𝅮 𝅘𝅥𝅮𝅘𝅥𝅮 𝅘𝅥𝅮𝅘𝅥𝅮

Eighth notes may be notated singly with a stem and a flag:

♪ 𝅘𝅥𝅮 𝅘𝅥𝅮 ♪

Or they may be beamed together in groups:

𝅘𝅥𝅮𝅘𝅥𝅮 𝅘𝅥𝅮𝅘𝅥𝅮 𝅘𝅥𝅮𝅘𝅥𝅮𝅘𝅥𝅮𝅘𝅥𝅮

8.2 Rhythm Builder

Read each line (clap, tap, or chant).

8.3 Sight-Read

Tr. #17 The Kangaroo

for 2-Part Speech Chorus*

Traditional

Music by
JOHN LEAVITT

*Accompaniment CD provides 3 beats of clicks before music begins.

8.4 The Dominant Chord

A *triad* is a special type of three-note chord built in thirds over a *root tone*. Following are some examples of triads.

Triads

When a *triad* is built on the keynote (or first degree) of a major scale, it is called a *tonic chord*. In tonal music, pitches and chords have relationships with each other. Some pitches and chords create a sense of resolution (at ease, rest) while others create a sense of momentum (movement or energy). The tonic chord creates a sense of resolution.

The *dominant chord* is a triad built on the fifth degree of a major scale. The dominant chord is perhaps the strongest chord of momentum, generally wanting to return home to the tonic.

G Major

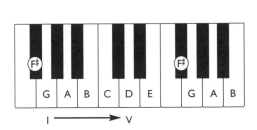

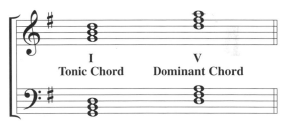

8.5 Chord Drills

Practice the following drills which outline the G major tonic and dominant chords. Remember, when the melody outlines the chord, you are singing melodic intervals. When three or more parts sing the pitches of the chord simultaneously, the ensemble is singing a chord.

8.6 Sight-Read

 Skip to My Lou

for SATB, a cappella

Arranged by
EMILY CROCKER

Traditional Game Song

8.7 Sight-Read

Tr. #19 The Three Rogues

for SATB, a cappella*

Arranged by
EMILY CROCKER

Traditional English

Brightly

Soprano
Alto

Unis. *f*

There was a might-y king, there was a might-y

Tenor
Bass

Unis. *f*

There was a might-y king, there was a might-y

king, and he had three sons run out of town be-

king, he had three sons, but

cause they could not sing. Be-cause they could not

oh, they could not sing.

sing, and he had three sons run

be-cause they could not sing, he

out of town be-cause they could not sing.

had three sons, but oh, they could not sing.

*Accompaniment CD provides 3 beats of clicks before music begins.

8.8 Sight-Read

Hush, Little Baby
for SATB and Piano

Arranged by
JOHN LEAVITT

Traditional

9.1 Key of F Major

The key of F major indicates that the keynote will be F. The staff below shows the F major scale as well as the whole/half step progression that is required for a major scale.

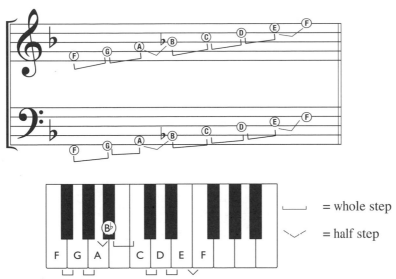

In F major, the whole/half step progression requires a B♭. (Remember that a flat lowers a pitch by one half step). If we had written A-B, the interval between these two pitches would have been a whole step rather than the required half step.

Remember also that a key signature is placed after the clef sign at the beginning of a line. This time the flat is on B's line, and it indicates that every time B occurs in the music, it should be sung as a B♭.

Key Relationships

So far, we've studied three major keys: C, G, and F. C major has no sharps or flats. G major has one sharp, F♯, and F major has one flat, B♭. G major and F major are considered neighboring keys to C major because the difference in the key signatures is only one note. Notice that G major (a sharp key) lies an interval of a fifth *higher* than C, and F major (a flat key) lies an interval of a fifth *lower* than C.

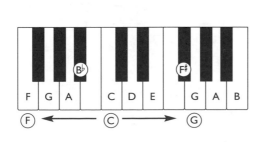

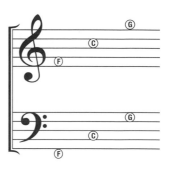

9.2 Chord Drills

Practice the following drills which outline the F major tonic and dominant chords.

I (Tonic) V (Dominant)

I (Tonic)

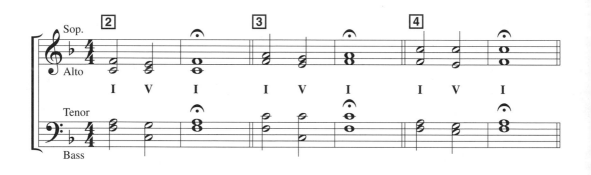

Sop.

Alto

Tenor

Bass

I V I   I V I   I V I

I V I

9.3 Pitch Builder

Sing each line separately and in any combination.

9.4 Sight-Read

Tr. #22 Hosanna In Excelsis Deo

for 4-Part Canon, a cappella

Edited by
JOHN LEAVITT

Adapted from
WOLFGANG AMADEUS MOZART

10.1 The Subdominant Chord

The *tonic chord* is a triad built on the keynote or first degree of a major scale. The *dominant chord* is a triad built on the fifth degree of a major scale.

The *subdominant chord* is a triad built on the fourth degree of a major scale.

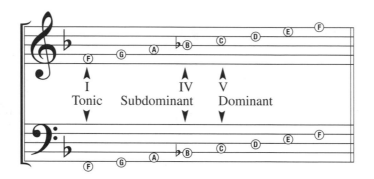

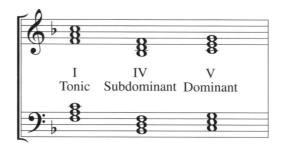

We've discussed the relationship of the tonic and dominant chords. In adding the subdominant chord, here is a description of the chords.

Tonic - at rest, at ease, home
Subdominant - digression or departure (away from the tonic)
Dominant - energy, momentum or movement (toward the tonic)

NOTE: The subdominant degree of the scale and the subdominant chord borrow their name from the dominant. If the dominant lies a fifth higher than the tonic, the *sub*dominant lies a fifth lower than the tonic.

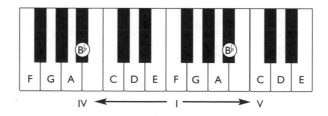

10.2 Chord Drills

Practice the following drills which outline the F major tonic, dominant and subdominant chords.

10.3 Pitch Builder

Sing each line separately and in any combination.

10.4 Sight-Read

 Set Me As a Seal

for SATB, a cappella

Text from
SONG OF SOLOMON 8:6-7

Music by
JOHN LEAVITT

11.1 Key of D Major

The key of D major indicates that the keynote will be D. The staff below shows the D major scale as well as the whole/half step progression that is required for a major scale.

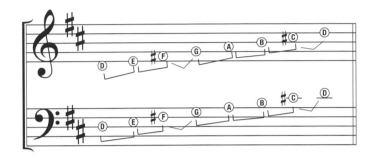

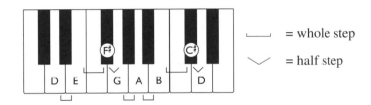

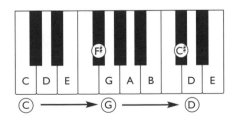

= whole step

= half step

In D major, the whole/half step progression requires an F♯ and a C♯. If we had written F-G and C-D, the intervals between each set of pitches would have been a whole step rather than the required half step. Thus, the key signature for D major is F♯ and C♯ (in that order).

Key Relationships

Remember that G major, which has one sharp, F♯, lies an interval of a fifth higher than C major (which has no sharps or flats). D major, which has two sharps, F♯ and C♯, lies a fifth higher than G major.

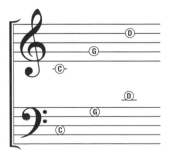

11.2 Chord Drills

Practice the following drills which outline the D major tonic, dominant and subdominant chords.

11.3 Pitch Builder

Sing each line separately and in any combination.

11.4 Sight-Read

Tr. #26 See Them Dance

(Les Petites Marionettes)

for SATB, a cappella

Arranged by
EMILY CROCKER

French Game Song

12.1 Sixteenth Notes and Rests

A *sixteenth note* (♪) is half the value of an eighth note. Two sixteenth notes (♫) have the same duration as one eighth note. The sixteenth note has a corresponding rest, the sixteenth rest (𝄿), which shares the same length as a sixteenth note.

Below is a chart summarizing the notes and rests we've learned.

	notes	rests
whole	o	▬
half	♩	▬
quarter	♩	𝄽
eighth	♪	𝄾
sixteenth	♬	𝄿

The following diagram summarizes the relationships between the notes we've studied:

If the quarter note receives the beat, you can consider eighth notes to be a *division* of the beat and sixteenth notes to be a *subdivision* of the beat:

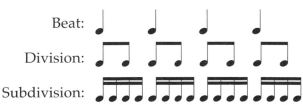

Sixteenth notes may be notated singly with a stem and a flag:

Or they may be beamed together in groups:

12.2 Rhythm Builder

Read each line (clap, tap, or chant).

12.3 Sight-Read

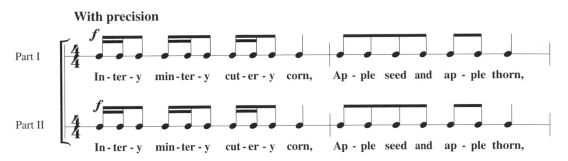

Tr. #27 Intery Mintery

for 2-Part Speech Chorus

Arranged by
EMILY CROCKER

Traditional Counting-out Rhyme

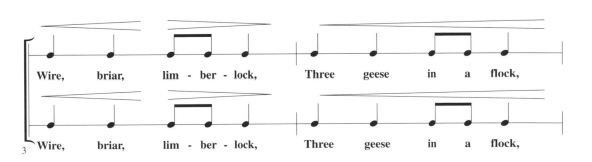

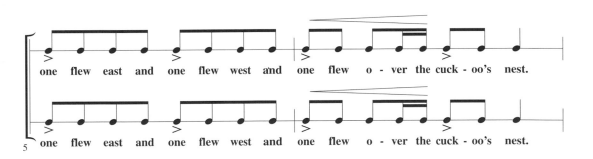

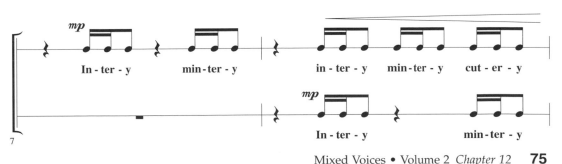

12.4 Sight-Read

Tr. #28 The Jumblies

for 2-Part Speech Chorus†

Words by
EDWARD LEAR (1812-1888)

Music by
JOHN LEAVITT

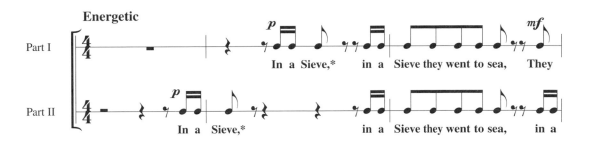

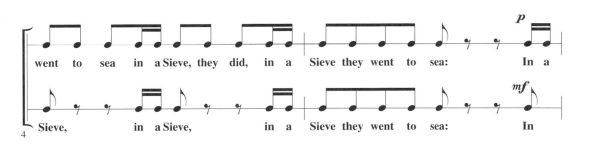

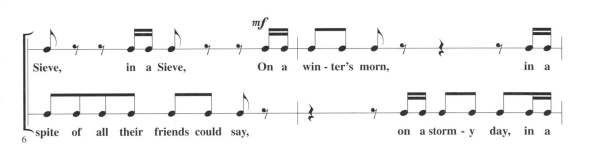

* *pronounced "sihv"*

†Accompaniment CD provides 4 beats of clicks before music begins.

12.5 Pitch Builder

Sing each line separately and in any combination.

12.6 Sight-Read

Tr. #30 **Cripple Creek**

for SATB and Piano

Arranged by
EMILY CROCKER

Game Song, adapted

Soprano

Goes up to see her 'bout the

Alto

Goes up to see her 'bout the

Tenor

John-ny's got a gal at the head of the creek,

Bass

John-ny's got a gal at the head of the creek,

13.1 Key of B♭ Major

The key of B♭ major indicates that the keynote will be B♭. The staff below shows the B♭ major scale as well as the whole/half step progression that is required for a major scale.

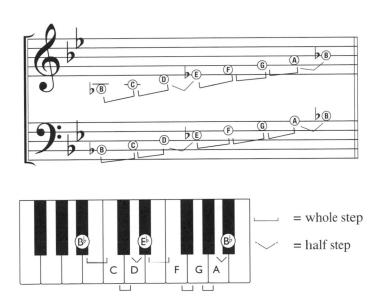

In B♭ major, the whole/half step progression requires a B♭ and an E♭. If we had written D-E and A-B, the intervals between each set of pitches would have been a whole step rather than the required half step. Thus, the key signature for B♭ major is B♭ and E♭ (in that order).

Key Relationships

Remember that F major, which has one flat, B♭, lies an interval of a fifth lower than C major (which has no sharps or flats). B♭ major, which has two flats, B♭ and E♭, lies a fifth lower than F major.

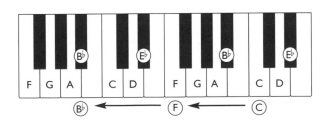

13.2 Chord Drills

Practice the following drills which outline the B♭ major tonic, dominant and subdominant chords.

13.3 Pitch Builder

Sing each exercise separately and in any combination.

Tr. #31

13.4 Sight-Read

 It Was a Lover and His Lass

for SATB, a cappella*

Text by
WILLIAM SHAKESPEARE

Music by
JOHN LEAVITT

*Accompaniment CD provides 2 beats of clicks before music begins.

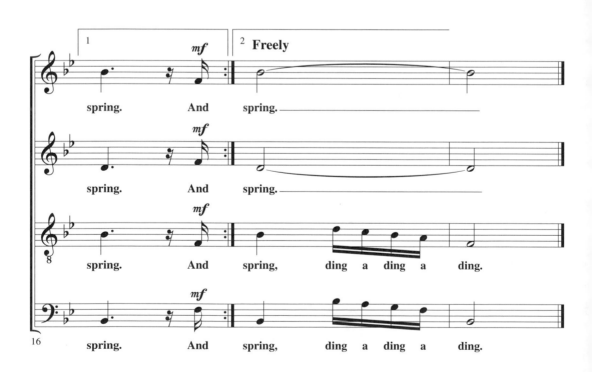

14.1 Natural Minor Scale

In addition to the major scale, one of the most common scales is the natural minor scale. A *natural minor scale* is a specific arrangement of whole and half steps in the following order:

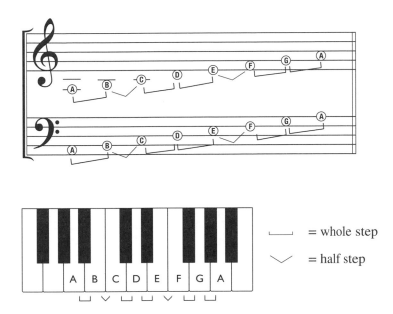

The chief difference between the major and minor scale is the third degree of the scale. In the natural minor scale, the third degree is a half step lower than the major scale. You will notice this difference in the quality of the sound of the scale.

14.2 Natural and Relative Minor Scales

Natural minor scales share the same key signature with a corresponding major scale. These are called *relatives*. The relative minor is always the sixth degree of the major scale. For example, both C major and A minor have no sharps or flats. G major and E minor each have one sharp. F major and D minor each have one flat.

Here are some major scales with their relative minors. Practice singing each scale.

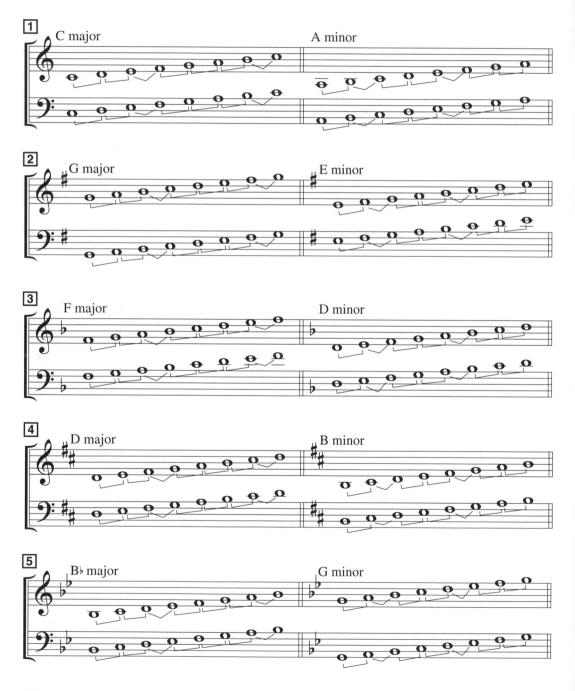

14.3 Pitch Builder

Look at the key signature and determine the key for each exercise. Then, sing each exercise in your own octave.

14.4 Sight-Read

 Fog

for SATB, a cappella

Text by
CARL SANDBURG

Music by
JOHN LEAVITT

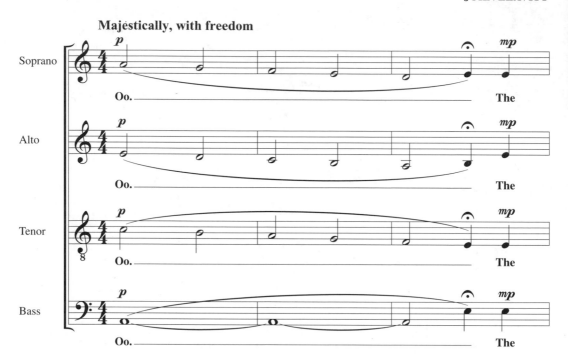

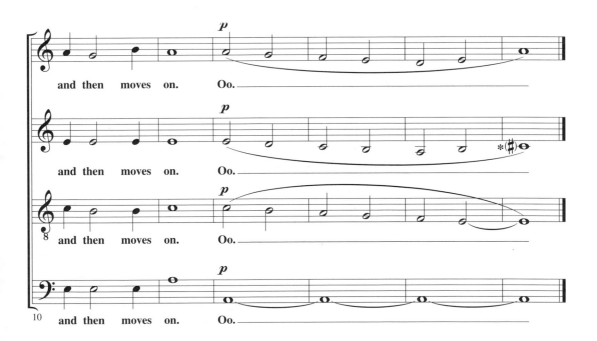

*optional raised third

15.1 Ties and Slurs

Ties and slurs appear as curved lines that connect notes or groups of notes, but they serve very different functions.

A *tie* connects two notes of the same pitch in order to extend duration. The first note is played or sung and held through the tied second note. See the example below.

A *slur* is a curved line that connects two or more notes with the purpose to play or sing them smoothly (legato). See the example below.

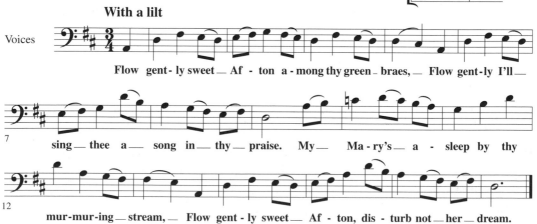

15.2 Rhythm and Pitch Builder

Read each line below to practice using ties (clap, tap or chant).

Sing the example below to practice using slurs.

Freu dich des Lebens

for 2-Part Canon

LUDWIG VAN BEETHOVEN

15.3 Dotted Notes and Rhythms

Remember that the duration of a note can be enlarged by adding a dot to the right of the notehead. The rule for a dotted note is that the dot receives half the value of the note (or rest).

Sometimes rhythms have unequal divisions or subdivisions of the beat. Let's quickly review *beat, division,* and *subdivision* as illustrated below.

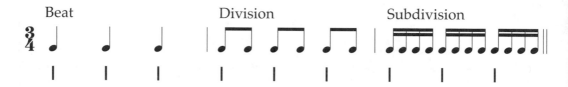

Dotted rhythms commonly occur as a dotted note followed by a shorter note value as illustrated below.

Practice

Read the example below (clap, tap or chant).

1

Now sing this rhythm!

2

Mu - sic when ——— soft voic-es die vi - brates in the mem-o - ry;

15.4 Rhythm Builder

Read each line (clap, tap, or chant).

15.5 Sight-Read

Tr. #34 Jeremiah Obadiah

for 2-Part Speech Chorus

Words: Anonymous

Music by
JOHN LEAVITT

Go to the "f" consonant blowing through fermata.

15.6 Sight-Read

Tr. #35 O Mankind

for SATB, a cappella

Text:
15th Century Anonymous

Music by
EMILY CROCKER

O _____ man-kind, _____ Have in thy mind my pas - sion smart. And thou _____ shalt _____ find _____ me full _____ kind, Lo! here _____ in _____ my _____ heart, my heart.

* optional raised third

15.7 Sight-Read

Tr. #36 Sing a Song of Sixpence

for SATB and Piano

Arranged by
JOHN LEAVITT

Traditional Words and Melody

Solfège

Movable Do

"Do" changes as the key changes.

Key of C Major

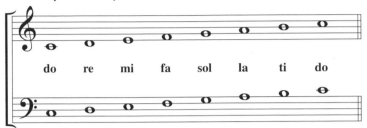

do re mi fa sol la ti do

Key of G Major

do re mi fa sol la ti do

Accidentals change as the key changes.

Ascending Chromatics ("do" changes in each key)

do (di) re (ri) mi fa (fi) sol (si) la (li) ti do

Descending Chromatics ("do" changes in each key)

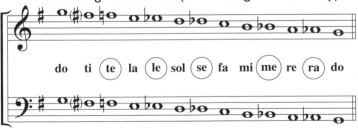

do ti (te) la (le) sol (se) fa mi (me) re (ra) do

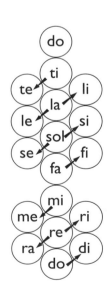

Solfège

Fixed Do

"Do" is C, and the pitch syllables remain fixed no matter what the key.

Key of C Major

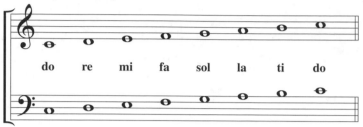

do   re   mi   fa   sol   la   ti   do

Key of F Major

fa   sol   la   te   do   re   mi   fa

"Do" is C, and accidentals remain fixed no matter what the key.

Ascending Chromatics

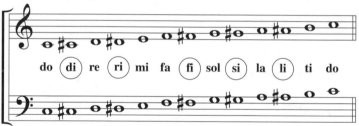

do (di) re (ri) mi fa (fi) sol (si) la (li) ti do

Descending Chromatics

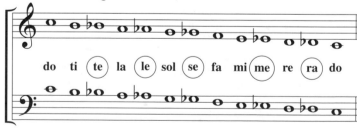

do ti (te) la (le) sol (se) fa mi (me) re (ra) do

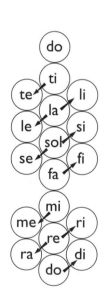

Numbers

Like movable "do," the "1" changes with each key.

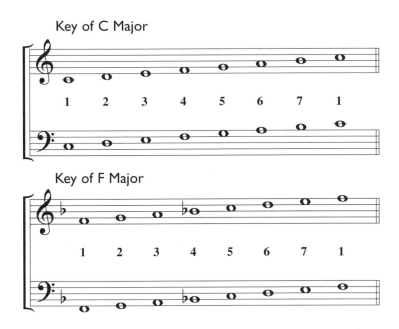

Accidentals can be performed either by singing the number but raising or lowering the pitch by a half step, or by singing the word "sharp" or "flat" before the number as a grace note.

Counting Systems

The Kodály System

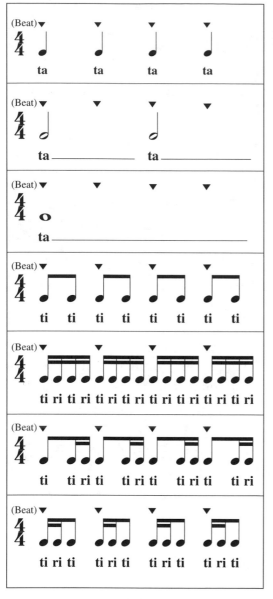

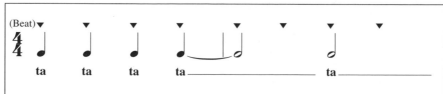

Counting Systems

The Traditional System

Counting Systems

The Eastman System

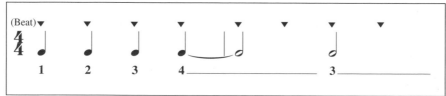

Other Simple Meters

Simple meters are based upon the note which receives the beat, i.e. $\frac{4}{4}$ meter is based upon the quarter note receiving the beat.

Adapt the information from the charts on pages 110-112 to apply to music in other simple meters:

2 = Two beats per measure (♪ ♪).
8 = The eighth note (♪) receives the beat.

3 = Three beats per measure (♪ ♪ ♪).
8 = The eighth note (♪) receives the beat.

4 = Four beats per measure (♪ ♪ ♪ ♪).
8 = The eighth note (♪) receives the beat.

2 – Two beats per measure (♩ ♩).
2 = The half note (♩) receives the beat. (Note: sometimes written as ¢ "cut time").

3 = Three beats per measure (♩ ♩ ♩).
2 = The half note (♩) receives the beat.

4 = Four beats per measure (♩ ♩ ♩ ♩).
2 = The half note (♩) receives the beat.

Compound Meter

Compound meters are meters which have a multiple of 3, such as 6 or 9 (but not 3 itself). Unlike simple meter which reflects the note that receives the beat, compound meter reflects the note that receives the division.

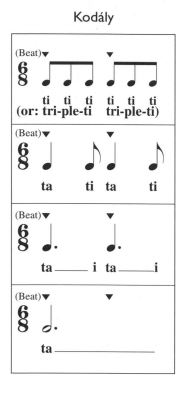

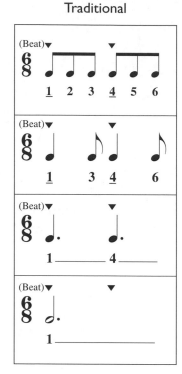

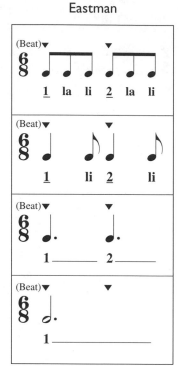

Other Compound Meters

Adapt the information from the above charts to apply to music in other compound meters.

To determine the note that receives the beat, add three divisions together. For example:

6 = Six divisions per measure (♫♫ ♫♫).
8 = The eighth note (♪) receives the division, dotted quarter note (♩.) receives the beat.

9 = Nine divisions per measure (♫♫ ♫♫ ♫♫).
8 = The eighth note (♪) receives the division, dotted quarter note (♩.) receives the beat.

12 = Twelve divisions per measure (♩♩♩ ♩♩♩ ♩♩♩ ♩♩♩).
4 = The quarter note (♩) receives the division, dotted half note (♩.) receives the beat.

An exception to this compound meter rule is when the music occurs at a slow tempo, then the music is felt in beats, rather than divisions.